PETER ROSE

PETER ROSE   HOUSES

PRINCETON ARCHITECTURAL PRESS, NEW YORK

PUBLISHED BY
Princeton Architectural Press
37 East Seventh Street
New York, New York 10003

For a free catalog of books,
call 1 800 722 6657.

Visit our website at
www.papress.com.

EDITOR
Lauren Nelson-Packard

DESIGNER
Jeff Ramsey

SPECIAL THANKS TO
Nettie Aljian, Bree Anne Apperley,
Sara Bader, Nicola Bednarek, Janet
Behning, Becca Casbon, Carina Cha,
Tom Cho, Penny (Yuen Pik) Chu,
Carolyn Deuschle, Russell Fernandez,
Pete Fitzpatrick, Wendy Fuller, Jan
Haux, Clare Jacobson, Erin Kim,
Aileen Kwun, Linda Lee, Laurie
Manfra, John Myers, Katharine Myers,
Dan Simon, Andrew Stepanian,
Jennifer Thompson, Paul Wagner,
Joseph Weston, and Deb Wood of
Princeton Architectural Press
—Kevin C. Lippert, publisher

Library of Congress
Cataloging-in-Publication Data

Peter Rose: houses. — 1st ed.
p. cm.
Includes bibliographical references.
ISBN 978-1-56898-821-4 (alk. paper)
1. Rose, Peter, 1943—Criticism
and interpretation. 2. Architecture,
Domestic—United States.
3. Architecture—United
States—History—20th century.
4. Architecture—United States—
History—21st century.
I. Rose, Peter, 1943-
NA749.R67A4 2010
728.092—dc22

2009032669

CONTENTS

FOREWORD
RAFAEL MONEO

The design of a single family house is one of the most daring and complicated jobs for an architect to assume. It is a challenge that touches on some of the most pregnant issues in architecture. Inevitably, it is an expression through architecture about how we would like to live. In fact, architects are rarely engaged with architecture as articulately as when they are designing a single family house. Almost every aspect of the design implies profound and intimate details about how we live. With other commissions—the design of a library, a hospital, a school, or a dorm—an architect works within the relatively familiar boundaries of building type and client expectations. Whoever has worked for an institution knows that they are run by people intent on describing how their buildings should be or even how they should look. The architect provides an image for the institution and the institution accepts this interpretation by the architect as part of the architect's contribution. The architect's knowledge is required and a certain degree of interaction between the architect and the client happens in a rather conventional process. Of course, architects, when designing, are projecting their *weltanschung*—the familiar German concept that is the expression of our world view—and they suspect that their *weltanschung* is shared by their clients.

I would say that the design of a single family house proceeds in a similar way: An individual or a couple entrusts an architect to offer an expression of how they would like to live. But this request also depends not just on how people want to live, but also on how they would like to be perceived. A house can tell more about us than the clothes we wear, the car we drive, or any other accessories. How should we proceed when making such a personal commitment? We could answer this question by saying that whoever wants a home chooses the architect with whom they feel closest, but that view is too optimistic. The relationship between architects and clients is more unpredictable. The most important ingredient for a successful design is the ability of the architect to inform the work with a psychological understanding of what the clients seek. It is a long process that brings the architect to the most sensitive interpretation of the client's personality, to discover how his or her skills can be useful in creating the desired home. Skills are not enough and it often requires a personal journey to discover a means of satisfying the client without betraying professional ideas. Indeed, it is a challenge that few architects handle well.

I will say that Peter Rose is one of the few architects I know who has succeeded. The group of houses published here reveals his ability to approach commissions in different conditions, and clients with widely diverse—even disparate—ideas of life. And yet, even though the houses are quite different— from Connecticut to Vermont, from Manhattan to Martha's Vineyard—they share something in common. They are always sensible to the landscape and the site. The house in Vermont makes arrival an occasion for celebrating nature. It becomes the retreat, the place where one reaches a sense of solitude that liberates us from daily life. The same could be said of the Martha's Vineyard house, where the chimneys and the roof promise protection in a landscape where uninterrupted flatness reminds us constantly of the ocean's proximity. The compound in Connecticut speaks to the hope of finding pleasure in activity, making the studio the protagonist of the ensemble. But the sense that the architect serves the wishes of urbanites escaping from the city remains as a leitmotif, always introducing the countryside as a sought after, idealized relief. Houses are then a lively world, which explains how the architect makes use of the encounter with nature away from the city. Strategically located windows are always present to offer wonderful views of the trees, cliffs, ponds, or the ocean. To be comfortable in the house seems to be the goal of the architect and in return he offers it as a gift to his clients/friends. In contrast, we see how his Manhattan house has tested his belief in an architecture that enjoys spaces and which makes the architectural promenade an opportunity to see the house as a frame for life. It is a frame which the owner offers to his guests, celebrating the social atmosphere of the city.

Rose is aware of how materials create architectural atmosphere and he works without altering them, presenting them in the most direct and natural way. Materials are varied but wood prevails, as well as concrete block, bricks, stone, and fine metals, untreated whenever possible so as to avoid the artificial. In construction they are handled with extreme care, with an extraordinary respect for the rational, suppressing things unexpected, seemingly in an attempt to prevent the clients/friends from making unwanted effort to change their lives with new habits, new uses, or new images. The result of this respect for materials leads to the right scale, where everything is handled without creating stress, without creating unwanted forces in the private world that the house becomes.

Rose achieves commendable results while keeping alive his broader interest in architecture. It has been said before, but it is worth repeating that the single family house is a laboratory for architects; it allows architects to test their architectural principles. That obviously happens in the case of Rose's collection of houses. His vision of buildings as a sequence of events and episodes reveals his mastery in articulating them with a sense of unity, in spite of a diverse set of conditions. Lastly, these houses allow Rose to engage in the design of objects, whether a lamp, a wall of shelves, a table, a handrail, a mantle, or a door handle. The pleasure and quality in the tactile nature of these elements is something that Rose enjoys. Behind all these works, there is a valuable set of architectural proposals already present in his other larger buildings, and I anticipate that the rich experience these houses show will accompany him in his future work.

Bottom detail at corner of operable window

PREFACE

PETER ROSE

INSTRUMENTS IN THE LANDSCAPE
EARLY INFLUENCES

The houses in this book span almost two decades of practice. While common threads can be found in the thinking that informed each design, the works also represent an evolution of my ideas, interests, confidence, and skills over time.

Much of what is basic to these houses comes out of interests and values I developed growing up in Quebec, both in the extraordinary city of Montreal and in the powerful Quebec landscape, and later at Yale University, especially the Architecture School. The aspects of the work that one might describe as beyond basic, even refined, were learned slowly, "on the job" over the course of many years of practice, and also teaching at Harvard University's Graduate School of Design.

When I was growing up in Montreal, I understood that buildings were critical places of activity, repose, and shelter. I also saw them as secondary to the landscape itself. My sense of the city was the same in that I generally believed individual buildings to be integral parts of a larger, more important whole. These are views I continue to hold today, views that inform the work in this book.

I am convinced that my thinking as a designer was profoundly shaped by three specific sets of experiences during my childhood: summers and weekends spent in a house my grandfather had built in 1918 on a lake seventy miles southeast of Montreal; time during the school year in Montreal itself; and winters in the mountains as a downhill ski racer.

THE HOUSE ON THE LAKE

The family house sits on the eastern shore of Lake Memphremagog. Running in a north-south orientation, the lake is a mile wide and thirty-five miles long. The house, designed by my businessman grandfather together with the local builder, is a modest bungalow, with three small bedrooms, a living room, and small kitchen. Its most important feature is a porch with views in two directions across the water. "Magog," as we called the house, was a magical place to me as a child. The house itself is ordinary, even banal as a piece of architecture. It retains its magic for me today for reasons that may seem to have little to do with architecture directly, but, in fact, inform each house in this book.

The magic of Magog starts with the incredible piece of land my grandfather found and built on. It is the only piece of land for miles around, with a view of the lake, not only to the west but also to the southwest, over a twenty-mile expanse of water. While the western view is classic, especially at sunset, the southwestern one is even better, offering flickering glimpses throughout the day of backlit waves, of clouds, of giant sheets of water at the front edges of rain storms, of snow storms, and all manner of weather dragged up the lake each day by the prevailing southwesterly winds.

The house is sited to take advantage of the views. Its plan, far from brilliant, is simply sensible. The living room looks through large windows and doors onto the porch. The other rooms in the house are really secondary. The porch is its glory. It faces south, not directly out across the water, but down the lake toward the sun.

On foot, the house is approached along a beautiful descending path that winds through a dense stand of mature cedar trees. Water is glimpsed only fragmentarily until, at the house, the lake suddenly fills the view. Although there is a front door, in daytime almost everyone walks around to the side of the house to the porch. The pull of the light bouncing off the water, the sound of the waves against the shore, the smell, and the moisture in the air, are simply too strong to do anything else.

Beyond shelter, the Magog house serves as a means to be in and spatially activate a set of natural phenomena: weather, light, water, and sky. It is an instrument in the landscape that mediates our relationship to the land, to the seasons, to the elements, to ourselves.

THE CITY BETWEEN THE RIVER AND THE MOUNTAIN

Montreal is a particular and affecting place. The city was founded in 1642 on an island in the St. Lawrence River at the point beyond which it was no longer navigable because of treacherous and violent rapids. It is one of the oldest cities in North America and very much a tough, vibrant port city.

Montreal is defined by dualities. It is a city that exists in many conditions of "in between." It is a river city, but it has a substantial mountain at its center, so it is a mountain city as well. Bilingual and bicultural, the presence of English and French languages, cultures, architectures, and histories permeate its entire fabric. Very much a historic city, with large Quartiers that remain intact from the 1890s and early 1900s (favorite locations for movies set in the early twentieth century), it is still a city that fully embraces modernity. Gloriously hot in the summers, with temperatures often reaching into the 90s, the winters are fierce, with vast quantities of snow and ice and temperatures as low as -40 degrees Fahrenheit. In summer, the days are very long and the sun high in the sky. On December 21st, the sun is only 21 degrees above the horizon at noon.

As a consequence, or perhaps in spite of the climate, there is a richness and a liveliness to Montreal, and a ruggedness and resourcefulness as well. Of the vast inventory of exceptional buildings, many have been built to exacting standards of craftsmanship and durability, partly out of pride in the long traditions of these qualities, partly simply to deal with the difficult conditions of topography and weather. Never a wealthy city, Montreal has used its resources strategically, economically, and artistically. I admire these qualities.

SPACE IN MOTION

If the house on Lake Memphremagog introduced me to landscape, ski racing provided a different kind of knowledge of landscape and expanded that understanding in unexpected ways. From the house, mountains are objects in the landscape, majestic points of reference, but background elements nevertheless. In skiing, one is dramatically in and on the mountains. Mountains are foreground, and lakes are in the distance. Skiing is all about topography in winter. Downhill ski racing is not about experiencing space from a position of repose, but experiencing and under-standing space and materials—snow, ice and trees, effects of light and contour—while hurtling through that space as fast as possible.

Though the conditions are different, buildings are experienced through motion as well. The intense experience of synchronizing the movement of body and mind with terrain, while flying through space and across surfaces that are constantly and unexpectedly changing in texture, color, density, and contour—and the split second decisions required to successfully navigate through that constantly mutating matrix of space and time—have played an important role in my development as a designer.

YALE ARCHITECTURE SCHOOL

It was not until I attended Yale University, and lived on the extraordinary Yale campus as an undergraduate, that I began to see and understand buildings in more than a casual way. There, in some of the best courses I took, numerous faculty but especially Vincent Scully brought buildings alive as architecture. At Yale Architecture School, which was then under the chairmanship of Charles Moore, in Paul Rudolph's great Art and Architecture building, was the formal beginning of my endless process of thinking about design. I learned a great deal from Moore: to carefully look at, to see, and be thrilled by buildings (what a great place Yale was for that); to be political, to value history, to be bold, to take risks, and to design thoughtfully. Then began the hard part, finding my own voice as an archi tect.

THE PROJECTS: JOURNEYS AND EXPERIMENTS

The houses in this book represent many journeys and experiments, and much learning on the job. Though the houses are all highly individual, and specific to their sites, programs, and clients, common to each of them is an ongoing interest in and investigation of landscapes, sites, and topographies.

LANDSCAPES/SITES/TOPOGRAPHIES

Except in the case of the New York City project, my thinking about design for the houses in this book invariably began with the landscape. In part, this was simple recognition of the landscape as context for intentionally site-specific work. Equally important, however, is my long held view that these large landscapes are a part of a public realm that we designers have the political/ethical responsibility to protect. Regardless of property ownership and boundaries, I have regarded building these houses as private acts in public spaces and worked on them accordingly.

In these landscapes, the projects are located and spatially calibrated, very much in relation to view: looking out, with the goal of establishing an integral connection, and a blurring of boundaries, between interior space, and the colors, shapes, sounds, and smells of the landscapes beyond; looking back with an eye toward making the houses as visually discreet as possible.

The projects in Vermont, Connecticut, and both houses on Martha's Vineyard are focused on the engaging of distant mountain ranges, meadows in the middle ground, and ocean waves crashing on nearby shores, as part of the intimate experiences of each house. This drawing of extraordinary views in, and the intensity of the looking out, is intentionally a one-way process. The projects are carefully sited back from the edges of plateaus, strategically screened with trees, built of materials that are mostly in muted shades of grey. When one looks back from a distance, these houses are scarcely there.

In the landscapes of the northeast, one becomes acutely aware of the passage of time: through the movement of the sun in a single day, the wide range of temperatures, textures, and colors of the four seasons, and especially the powerfully changing weather. Being able to thrive in, adapt to, and profit from these changes was one of the defining goals of these projects.

The Vermont house in particular was thought of as a robust winter house first, capable of seeming safe and secure on a remote hilltop, in the middle of a raging winter blizzard, with winds of sixty miles per hour, thirty degrees below zero temperatures and three feet of snow. Sited in such a way as to be easily plowed after winter storms, the house and landscape undergo a series of gradual but beautiful transitions from winter through spring, summer, and fall. The landscape blooms and provides color and shade, helping to frame views, channel winds, and keep the house cool. The house gradually opens up, reversing its winter mode and letting the outside in. This process happens in a similar, if less extreme way for the Connecticut house. On Martha's Vineyard, the thinking process for both houses was the reverse. These are summer houses first, capable of being comfortable in the relatively mild island winters, but geared to being radically opened up, drawing to the breezes, sounds, and smells of the ocean shore, indeed the landscape itself, right into their interiors.

ABSTRACTION

Chronologically, the projects seem to move generally from representation toward abstraction, with the house in Vermont being most recognizably part of a vernacular tradition, the concrete house on Martha's Vineyard being the most abstract, and the house in Connecticut somewhere in between.

I am not sure I understand how the forces pull one toward representation and/or abstraction work. The Vermont project began with the idea that it should be a legible piece of the local vernacular. This was my way of being respectful in a fragile and beautiful landscape, a landscape where vulgar "mansions" had been upsetting the order and scale of things. Beginnings aside, the Vermont project, in its plans, materials, details, and tectonics is far from a typical vernacular house. From the concrete block exterior to the wood plank, plywood veneer, and steel interiors, there is hardly a molding or a symmetry in sight. It is in this house that I began, quite subconsciously I think, to investigate and gently move toward abstraction.

The evidence of an ongoing investigation of abstraction is in all the houses, unequivocally in the interiors, often partially concealed by vernacular references on the exteriors. The most abstract of all is the most recent project, the second Martha's Vineyard house. Isolated on a windy bluff, surrounded by a tenacious landscape of shrubs, low trees, and vines, abstraction (along with the use of concrete) was part of a strategy for making a house robust enough to hold its own in a rugged environment.

CONCLUSION

These projects were designed and built for exceptional clients who provided me in each case with extraordinary sites, more than adequate budgets, good taste, and thoughtful continuous collaboration—in short, every advantage I could have asked for. This is an acknowledgment both of good fortune, and of the fact that every substantial work of architecture is a collaboration between architect and client. In the end the projects were intensely personal, both for the clients and for me. The houses in this book represent a body of work of which I am both very fond and immensely proud.

PETER ROSE: HOUSES

WILLIAM MORGAN

The houses of Peter Rose are as much elements of the landscape they inhabit as the earth or the sky. A vacation house on a rocky island in Ontario's Georgian Bay epitomizes his understanding of the genius of the place. Like a Viking ship, the wooden house is the perfect combination of efficiency and strength—built to take on severe weather, but with a graceful economy of means. The orientation is more than chance, for it not only embraces the lake view and the sun, its back is to the prevailing winds. Simplicity and purpose make this house seem to have been on the bay for decades, at once timeless and as fresh as the coming summer.

It is the creating of houses that best reveals a designer's true center. Even though Rose has had a distinguished career as a teacher, planner, and architect, his houses are where he most experiments. As a rule, homes are for a single client, programmatically demanding, and intensely personal. The house has long been a laboratory, the place where every thoughtful architect—whether Aalto, Koolhaas, or Zumthor, Palladio, Jefferson, or Lutyens—tries out ideas.

The five houses featured in this book represent an exquisitely refined evolution of domestic architecture. While the Georgian Bay house is an homage to the gurus of Rose's Yale architectural education—Charles Moore and Robert Venturi—the more recent domestic work has moved far beyond the simplicity of the figural house-is-a-house form to a sophisticated astylar expression that is purely and confidently Peter Rose. The lessons learned from teachers and earlier houses, as well as admiration for heroes such as C. F. A. Voysey and Sigurd Lewerentz, have not been forgotten.

Only seven years after the Georgian Bay house, another vacation home shows a progression in the refinement of Peter Rose's domestic design. This getaway for a Montreal couple is nestled into a gentle slope on the side of Mount Worcester in Vermont, taking in a westerly view of the Green Mountains. As a native of neighboring Quebec, the architect was temperamentally suited to designing for northern New England's four dramatically different seasons. Here, Rose worked with Dan Kiley, America's preeminent Modern landscape architect, and together they created a meandering approach to the house that culminates in a protective courtyard of house, guesthouse, and garage. The attached units recall the vernacular spirit of the New England connected house-shed-barn configuration. The spirits of both the Cape Cod cottage and the early French farmsteads of the St. Lawrence River Valley are adopted here and further emphasized by the two-over-two farmhouse windows, and especially by the sheltering roof-to-wall ratio of the main house. Rose's introduction of concrete block and horizontal cedar clapboards strengthens the sense of rural informality.

At the Vermont house, the units of house, guest quarters, and supporting structures are part of the meadow landscape, as if they had developed naturally over the years to serve farmers whose concerns were utilitarian rather than stylistic. Nevertheless, the spreading plan is definitely not merely agricultural, demonstrating Rose's exploration of subtler, non-figural relationships with living spaces.

<u>PETER ROSE: HOUSES</u>
WILLIAM MORGAN

Island residence, Georgian Bay, Ontario,
west facade

Mountain residence, concrete block
wall in multiple tones due to varied
concrete mixtures

The interior is decidedly contemporary with its hand-tinted plaster walls, exposed structural steel I beams, pipe railings, and dormers that act as skylights. Like all later Rose houses, the Stowe house is a *gesamtkunstwerk*. Rose designed all of the cabinetry, the drawer pulls and door handles, and the sinuous unadorned metal railing along the back stairs. Obsessed with the tactile qualities of shadow, Rose incorporated a sunscreen, shading the porch of gray Maine stone, providing a quiet moment as laden with meaning as a carefully chosen rock in a Zen garden.

But this should not distract from the underlying rationale of the plan, as Rose began to dissolve corners and make his plans more abstract. Like Frank Lloyd Wright, Peter Rose shapes space by varying ceiling heights and by manipulating axes, so the plan is fluid yet not immediately revealing. Spaces lead—doorless—from corners of rooms. The wooden ceiling of the dining room offers intimacy and enclosure in contrast to the living room's two-story height.

The experimentation Rose undertook at the country house in Vermont resonated in a more public commission, a school for Cranbrook, the remarkable academic community created by the Finnish architect Eliel Saarinen. Comprised of an art museum, a design school, and two secondary schools, Cranbrook combined the medievalism of William Morris's Kelmscott Manor with an industrial modernity.

Cranbrook Academy expanded its original Saarinen campus, hiring a cadre of unusually sensitive designers, such as Steven Holl, Tod Williams and Billie Tsien, and Rafael Moneo, as well as Juhani Pallasmaa. Yet Rose most understood that Saarinen was arguably the only real competitor to Wright in terms of melding the Arts and Crafts aesthetic with Modernism.

Rose captured the true sense of Cranbrook: the tinted concrete block, the wood detailing that evokes Scandinavian memories, and the Nordic classicism of relaxed formality. Still, the essence of the Rose classroom building is not a reference to past masters. The thoroughly successful design is the result of Rose's willingness to be a polite neighbor, to allow the landscape to shape the procession of spaces, and for the uses of the building to inform the program.

Further measures of Rose's ability to respect the giants upon whose shoulders he stands was his ingenious insertion of a new art gallery inside Harvard's Carpenter Center, Le Corbusier's only North American work. The Josep Lluís Sert Gallery (named for another European master in America), comprised of completely removable parts, was incorporated into the concrete building without marking it in any way. How many architects could resist the chance to work against Le Corbusier rather than with him?

As the recent houses by Peter Rose are part of a continuum, it is worthwhile to understand a little more about who Peter Rose is. Nominally, he is a Montreal-born, Yale-trained, Cambridge-based architect who has practiced for more than three decades and taught at Harvard for two. His work has ranged from museums and art studios to a master plan for the Montreal waterfront.

Rose may be best known for his brilliant design for the Canadian Centre for Architecture. This premier repository of architectural drawings and documents was a dream project. Rose's client was the architect Phyllis Lambert, who convinced her father to hire Mies van der Rohe to design the Seagram Building in New York. Lambert was equally determined to create a landmark with the

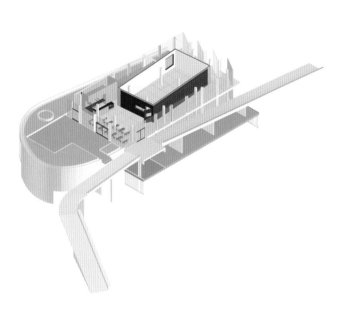

19   PETER ROSE: HOUSES
     WILLIAM MORGAN

Brookside Lower School, Cranbrook
Educational Community, Bloomfield
Hills, Michigan, main courtyard

Sert Gallery, Carpenter Center,
Cambridge, MA, view of partial 3D
model of ramp, lobe, and inserted steel
gallery box

Sert Gallery, Carpenter Center,
Cambridge, MA, close up of steel panel
wall

new home for the C.C.A. The young architect was allowed to experiment with a variety of materials; he constructed full-scale mock-ups of wall sections in different stones to observe how they responded to light in all seasons. Interior finishes, too, were accordingly lush—John Hejduk referred to the small auditorium there as "like the inside of a violin," where sound, materials, and space created the complete container.

Rose is deservedly proud of the C.C.A., and it is a near perfect institutional building. Yet, having this accomplishment so early in his career is a bit like a twenty-something actor winning an Oscar for his first film, or Lorin Maazel conducting the New York Philharmonic at the age of twelve. A success so early can inhibit maturation, so the C.C.A. was the masterpiece that the architect had to surpass. This, added to the perpetual dilemma of an artist in Canada: Does one stay at home and work modestly—that is, be Canadian, or does one pursue greater opportunities in the United States?

As successful as Rose has been in the United States, he was significantly shaped by his upbringing as an Anglophone in French-speaking Montreal, Canada's most cosmopolitan city. In lectures Peter Rose often introduces himself with an image of a Montreal street buried in snow. He follows this by another picture of a rural Quebec landscape with power lines barely protruding above the white mantle. So much white—and so much darkness—in the northern latitudes strongly affects light, shadows, and one's psyche.

Rose's mother was English (and the niece of Hewlett Johnson, the so-called "Red Dean" of Canterbury Cathedral), his father was a musician and a scien-

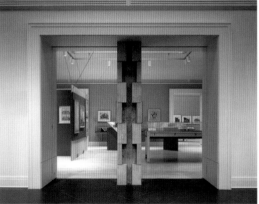

<u>HOUSES</u>   Canadian Centre for Architecture, Montreal, Quebec, close up, front facade   Canadian Centre for Architecture, Montreal, Quebec, exhibition gallery entry

tist, and also Jewish in politely anti-Semitic Montreal. Religion was never discussed in the Rose household, yet Peter's paternal grandparents were Russian immigrants whose name was no doubt shortened at customs and were part of the Diaspora. Mordechai Richler, chronicler of Jewish Montreal through characters like Duddy Kravitz and Joshua Shapiro, was a friend and summer neighbor of the Roses at Lake Memphramagog near the Vermont border.

Young Rose led a life of privilege. He attended Lower Canada College, where in the tradition of the English public school there was Latin, English history, and lots of sports. And it was athletics that proved Rose's saving grace and allowed him to escape family tensions. During the winter, Rose skied every day, learning self-confidence as well as skill.

Skiing provided a key for Rose's development as a visual person, as an architect. Although a good overall skier, it was the downhill that provided a personal breakthrough. Downhill skiing is faster than slalom, and there are no gates, just the trail. Rose was not stronger or more coordinated than his classmates, but downhill revealed a special gift: an ability to visualize space. Roaring down the trail, one can go faster by sensing the snow's texture and temperature, by mastering the changes in topography. Staying on one's skis and winning requires absolute clarity about the space through which one is moving. That intuition about space has remained with Rose as he internalizes the spirit of a place. The great skier and the confident architect must be able to frame the terrain.

It was this skiing expertise that tempted Peter Rose to forgo college to train for the Winter Olympics, where he was almost certain to gain a spot on the Canadian downhill team. He knew he did not want to follow the normal Anglo-Montrealer's path to McGill University. Looking south, Rose applied to Princeton and Yale and was accepted by both. Having seen neither campus, he decided on Yale because it had a ski team and was closer to the slopes.

As skiing saved Rose at Lower Canada College, architecture saved him at Yale. As captain of the Yale ski team, he faced a possible future as a ski bum. But it was the legendary "darkness at noon" history of art taught by the dramatic Vincent Scully that opened Rose's eyes to architecture. Legions of Yalies have been made better design patrons by Scully, but Rose went on to take more Scully offerings, and less of his proposed science major. These dovetailed with an enthralling drawing course with Sy Sillman, a protégé of Josef Albers, who was thus a link to the world of the Bauhaus.

The 1960s was a time of unrest at colleges and universities everywhere, perhaps more so at Yale, where, besides the Vietnam War, New Haven had radicals like the Black Panthers who fueled unrest and railed at urban sores. The Art and Architecture building, a New Brutalist composition by Paul Rudolph, was seen as a symbol of elitist, socially unresponsive design. After its mysterious burning— indubitably for political and not aesthetic reasons—Rose set up a studio in a store on Chapel Street.

Even more significant was the design revolution begun by architecture dean Charles Moore, an architect whose own work was characterized by Pop imagery and a return to vernacular sources. It was under Moore that visiting critic Robert Venturi, the guru of Post-Modernism, took a Yale seminar to study the neon and glitz strip in the Nevada desert, culminating in the seminal book *Learning from Las Vegas*. In keeping with heightened social awareness was the Yale building project that Moore instituted, wherein first-year graduate students had to leave the classroom and actually build something, preferably a structure to help the underprivileged. A number of students, Rose among them, went to New Zion in desperately poor Appalachian Kentucky to build a community center.

That modest civic structure was built of rough lumber and featured the shed roofs that were so much a part of the Charlie Moore aesthetic (best seen in the iconic second-home community Sea Ranch in northern California). Rose and his roommate Andrus Burr decorated their New Haven carriage house with homemade, painted plywood furniture in Moore's two-dimensional Pop Art style, while they upholstered the usual graduate student cast-off sofas in an army surplus felt designed to cushion jeeps in parachute drops.

The influence of Moore was far more than stylistic, for many members of the Yale Architecture Class of 1970 practiced architecture as an instrument of social policy. Designers like Daniel Scully, Roc Caivano, Turner Brooks, and Andy Burr continued to practice in an anything-worth-doing-is-possible counter-culture spirit. The crudely but aptly named "chainsaw houses" that Brooks and Burr erected in rural Vermont stand in strong contrast to the slick corporate approach of the major—and decidedly urban—firms of the day. With the exception of the classmate who made a fortune as the creator of Soap-on-a-Rope, most of the members of this class found spiritual fulfillment rather than fame.

Rose's master's thesis was an intriguing combination of these core Moore values and the old-fashioned Beaux-Arts *equisse*. Done in collaboration with James Righter, an older student who turned to architecture after Wall Street, the project was a development scheme for Copper Mountain ski resort on Colorado land owned by Righter's family. Copper Mountain was more than condominiums on a slope, as this design addressed the larger context of the entire town—people, buildings, and nature. Copper Mountain was a harbinger of Rose's future urban planning.

Rose had always planned to return to his hometown to practice. Plus, Montreal seemed to be on the cusp of a bright new era with the innovative and superbly managed world's fair, Expo 67. Calling themselves the Endless Construction Company, Rose and Andy Burr opened an office in Montreal.

Their first commission was a house for a McGill professor in the Eastern Townships of Quebec. The sprayed, structural polyurethane house reflected the restless spirit of their tutelage with Charles Moore. More overtly post-modern was the ski lodge built at Mont Saint-Sauveur; its Venturi-esque signifier facade served as the frontispiece of Charles Jencks's *The Language of Post-Modern Architecture*.

Peter Rose's very first house, however, was one he designed for himself while still at Yale. As he remembers, the small retreat he designed on his parents' property in Magog was the product of "cockiness and complete uncertainty"—both cool and naive. Designed as it was being built over a year in the late 1960s, the shed-roof and raw-wood vertical-sided house was very much an echo of the work of Moore. Rose punched holes before he knew what windows might be available—a lot of windows were recycled, as were the bricks for the chimney. Yet he learned a lot on this modest project, not least of all how to orient the house to the land, and the Magog house, with its uncertain elevations, was the start of Rose's refining the dimensions of the house.

Hugging the mountainous spine of western New England and equally as much a landscape composition as domestic architecture, is a house and studio in Sharon, Connecticut. Constructed almost three decades after his first house, Rose laid out a circuitous approach that takes the visitor past a grove of trees, revealing the house only at the last moment. Or rather, one sees only the concrete block wall of the courtyard (formed by house, guesthouse/garage, and artist's studio). The landscape opens beyond the enclave; the courtyard and its defining buildings act as a stage set, a sort of belvedere from which to contemplate twenty-mile views of the Taconic Hills. Like an unfolding Japanese scroll or a stroll through a Picturesque English garden, the Sharon house shapes and defines the viewer's interaction with the land. The questioning dialogue with the landscape begun at Magog is almost fully resolved.

The iconic, seemingly casual but carefully directed journey is shaped inside by ceiling heights and the use of different materials. Comprised of rectangular blocks divided by a full-length hallway that allows revelatory glimpses of the landscape at either end, the interior is further connected with outside. The laminated "starfire" glass hall table and the slatted staircase "banisters" above it are tributes to the quiet but inventive tours-de-force that make a Rose house such a tactile and visual delight. Changing as one moves up the stairs, the slats create an optical rhythm. This could also be a metaphor for the layered and laminated plan of the house—a major evolution from the Vermont house of just half a dozen years earlier.

It is almost hard to imagine the sophisticated and assured Sharon studio-home as being by the same designer as the freshly minted architect's summer cottages on Lake Memphramagog. Back then, too, Rose and Andy Burr were increasingly involved in urban projects, including building some giant inflatable bubbles of industrial polyethylene and packing tape. The desire to be more involved with the city and with larger architectural issues led Rose to establish a lecture series, which in turn landed him the most definitive commission of his early career.

With seed money from the Aluminum Company of Canada, Rose founded the Alcan Lectures in 1973. Bringing in several architects, artists, and historians annually, the popular public series ran for fifteen years and was an important voice in shaping the city's perceptions of design and urbanism. It also meant that Rose had contact with just about anyone of consequence in his profession (Philip Johnson was the only invitee who turned him down). Rose played host to an endless string of American designers such as Venturi, Peter Eisenman, and Michael Graves, as well as Europeans Alvaro Siza, Rem Koolhaas, and Rafael Moneo, along with the leading Japanese architects Tadao Ando, Arato Isozaki, and Fumihiko Maki. Phyllis Lambert was a regular attendee at the lectures and became acquainted with Rose at the dinners for the speakers afterward. She asked Rose to do some work for her, culminating in 1981 with the commission to design the C.C.A.

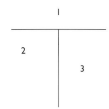

1

2

3

1 Art Studio and Residence, vista from entry court   2 Inflatable structure by Peter Rose, Montreal, Quebec   3 New York Townhouse, New York, NY, facade in springtime

Built at the same time as Paris's Centre Pompidou, the C.C.A. was the opposite of that contemporary art museum. It was dedicated neither to public entertainment nor unlimited accessibility. The very nature of collecting valuable and fragile works of art primarily on paper meant designing a mostly private repository based on a concern for light and humidity; large areas of the museum would not be open to the public. The new museum's classical forms and formal character were shaped by the fact that it was wrapped around an 1874 Second Empire–style mansion Phyllis Lambert had bought to save from the wrecking ball.

Since the mansion core of the museum was unsuitable for exhibitions, Rose transformed its rooms into spaces for Montrealers to gather for cultural events. His connection to an earlier Montreal became a touchstone for Rose, and the house was integral in creating progressive degrees of entry into the institution. Rose understood the house's symbolism in Montreal, and was able to insert the new museum into the city in a seamless manner. "The size, its placement, the materials, the classical language of it," Rose remarked, "the use of those axes are part of the way the city is organized, the lines that go through all the way from the river to the mountain—it's all part of a sense that I have acquired from looking at the house site for ten years."

The thoughtful exploitation of the glimpse of the outside or the next room is equally developed in a 1918 Beaux-Arts Manhattan townhouse that Rose recreated for Phyllis Lambert's nephew. Edgar Bronfman and his Venezuelan-born wife Clarissa wanted a family home, a place to display their art collection, and a grand space for entertaining. An entirely new house was constructed behind the Paris-in-New York limestone facade. The New York house is as equally well choreographed as the earlier C.C.A., while it continues the exploration of housing masterworks within an existing classical framework, here in a looser, less formal manner.

The house is built around a museum-like sky-lit atrium. The staircase clings to the walls, while the balconies that overlook it are like a stage set for an opera— a street turned in upon itself. The court ought to dominate the visitor's attention, yet it is the seemingly axis-free space, what Rose calls a "meander in the park," that enthralls. One has to climb a few stairs to reach the strikingly vertical court, but before one can look up, the eye is drawn to the dining room, and through it to the Dan Kiley-designed city garden beyond. Even the dining table was designed so that its narrow profile forms a line across the view. The Bronfman house is purely about the shaping of space, the historical references seen in the C.C.A. are left behind.

Along with accolades for the Montreal museum came the assumption that Rose's career was assured from this point on. This was a bump that potentially could have sent Rose off course. He also was concerned with how to prosper in an increasingly Separatist Quebec.

The inclusive spirit of Expo '67 evaporated with new French language laws, while hundreds of companies and thousands of Anglophones fled Montreal for Toronto, Vancouver, and the United States. Although apolitical, Rose was edged out for jobs by French-speaking firms or those with Parti Québecois connections. Rose and his wife, the architectural historian Eve Blau, were the parents of two young children and were concerned about the rising level of violence in the province. Radcliffe offered Blau a research fellowship and architecture chairman Rafael Moneo asked Rose to teach at Harvard, so the Roses moved to Cambridge in 1992.

Teaching is a constant in the shaping of a designer; architecture schools are the battlegrounds for ideas and the incubators of new movements. Rose had taught as a visiting critic at McGill, Toronto, and Princeton, but at Harvard's Graduate School of Design he became a permanent member of a community of scholars and practitioners. In addition to working with his mentor Moneo, Rose has served under chairs Mack Scoggin, Jorge Silvetti, and Toshiko Mori.

Rose was a logical choice for a thoroughly green project on another academic setting, Milton Academy. The high school science building for the venerable New England prep school would have brought a new type of laboratory teaching space to the heart of this Georgian campus, one designed to cool and heat itself. Composed of two wings around an atrium that would have been part of a major school pathway, the Science Building featured catwalks across the interior street, connecting the hybrid "classlabs." Having put mechanicals in an overhead spine, the particularly transparent walls were even more open to reconfiguration. The evolution of Rose's designs from the C.C.A. and Cranbrook to Milton echo a parallel development in the houses wherein a focus on true function and general livability has long overshadowed any attempt at an envelope designed merely to please or impress.

A 10,000-square-foot retreat that Rose built in Big Sky, Montana, would seem a logical exercise for either client or architect hubris. Rose took his cue from the Rocky Mountain setting. He tamed the large house by inserting it into a steeply sloping hillside and fracturing the plan so that a number of smaller elements mitigate an otherwise potentially massive structure. This heliotropic plan seeks the sun while providing a range of spectacular views of the alpine landscape. Employing quarried local stone and cedar boards, Rose offered an alternative to the usual second-home-in-Montana clichés of varnished knotty pine and huge boulder-strewn walls.

How could one not be seduced by the drama of the New York museum-house and the landscapes that become part of the houses in the Rockies, the Litchfield Hills, and the Green Mountains? This is even truer at Chilmark on Martha's Vineyard, where Rose placed a weekend cottage among the marsh grasses. It has views of the ocean from every room and corner windows roll back the boundaries between landscape and hearth. The Chilmark house offers the metaphors of shelter and freedom—a home that can weather a hurricane and casually serve as a stage for summer idyll.

The combination of openness and rootedness distantly recalls Wright, yet the choreographed approach to the house, and then inside, the sense of journey created by manipulating space, are thoroughly Peter Rose. Obsessive attention to materials and construction details are Rose hallmarks, but his primary design voice is spatial. Room uses are subtly demarcated through shifts of scale created by different floor levels and ceiling heights. Destinations like bedrooms and kitchens are suggested, not seen; glimpses of the Atlantic disappear and reappear. The corners of the windows can literally be rolled back and all but obliterated. Rose's Chilmark

<u>PETER ROSE: HOUSES</u>
WILLIAM MORGAN

2 Big Sky Residence, Big Sky, Montana, view of entry and landscape from terrace

3 Big Sky Residence, Big Sky, Montana, view of landscape from terrace and pool

4 Chilmark House, Martha's Vineyard, MA

work approaches the ideal of what a house should be: a contemplative work of art, as balanced and as harmonious as an Amish rocking chair or a well crafted short story.

If one of Rose's great strengths is a reductive distillation of the essence of a house, the next step in his domestic evolution might be Zen to the point of invisibility, and this house is even more abstract. East House (also in Chilmark) melds even more with the landscape, nestling into the characteristic island shrubbery above sixty-foot bluffs. Constructed of concrete, with grass roofs and geothermal heating, this getaway for a New York family is comprised of four blocks—two for sleeping and two less-private spaces with library, living, and kitchen areas. (These cubes are designed to be movable by crane in the event the bluffs erode.) The social consciousness of Charles Moore's shed-roofed vernacular has been reinvigorated and translated anew in twenty-first century terms.

The basic cubes flank an entranceway that becomes a corridor that becomes a courtyard that frames an ocean view. The complex is sited to heighten one's awareness of the wind and to capture sea breezes. The figural house is gone, replaced by the melding of house and landscape.

The Vineyard houses, like the other New England homes, carry neither the heavy burden of architectural polemic nor the psychological baggage of owner ego. Most of all they show Rose's critical experimentation over forty years: From the reverence for the vernacular and vertical spatial layering of his Yale training, to the understanding of city and landscape, to the tougher and edgier plans of the later houses, and to the total concern for process and materiality.

The Chilmark houses best demonstrate Rose's mature artistry, as they are composed of sumptuous materials and sensitive spaces. The houses of Peter Rose are understated masterpieces that add to our world. They remind us that good architecture is built upon tradition, is part of its place, and fulfills both functional and spiritual needs.

<u>PETER ROSE: HOUSES</u>
WILLIAM MORGAN

East House, Martha's Vineyard, MA, view of
seascape from living area, rendering

MOUNTAIN HOUSE

Defined by its great range in temperature, color, wind, smell, and humidity over four distinct and dramatic seasons, northern Vermont presents both opportunities and constraints. The design and construction of this house is a response to these qualities. The clients are a Montreal-based family who wanted both a retreat and a place to display contemporary art.

This 6,500 square-foot home in the hills surrounding Stowe, Vermont, is located in a clearing overlooking a small lake, with spectacular views of Mount Mansfield in the distance. Four buildings consisting of a main house, a small guest-house attached by a wood and glass portico, a detached garage, and a barn form a protected courtyard that serves as the main entry and focal point for the complex. Organized beneath broad sloping roofs, the house is intimately connected to its site, and the window openings and dormers are positioned to heighten the relationship between interior volumes and the landscape.

Great care has been taken to use natural materials and expressive detailing to harmonize with the surrounding natural landscape while maintaining simplicity and clarity of construction. The entire project uses wood framing, which includes spruce joists, rafters and studs; laminated Southern Yellow pine posts and beams; and Douglas fir rafter extensions and collar ties. The guesthouse incorporates similar details along with tongue and groove red cedar siding. Custom made mahogany windows and doors are used throughout the project, and lead-coated copper roofs, concrete block walls and brick chimneys complete the exterior material palette. On the interior, cherry tongue and groove and Douglas fir end-grain flooring, exposed fir collar ties, reverse board and batten Douglas fir ceilings, and mahogany casework compliment the exterior materials and accentuate the mostly plaster interior volumes.

The relationship between landscape and house is tied to the senses in carefully crafted details that integrate these materials. A foot scraper at the house entry signals the muddy environment for boots, and the transition from exterior to interior. Made of a single piece of cut steel, it advertises its purpose at a glance, and is of a similar construction to the much taller, thinner handrail next to it. Without a superfluous bend, the handrail traces the path the hand must take, and connects ground to step with a single line. Further afield, dry-set stone, occupying only a step or two, marks the transition from earth to wood-planked dock. To reach the dock, one walks from soft earth to stone, set like a foundation, and then reaches the light wood planks floating over water.

North elevation seen from lake

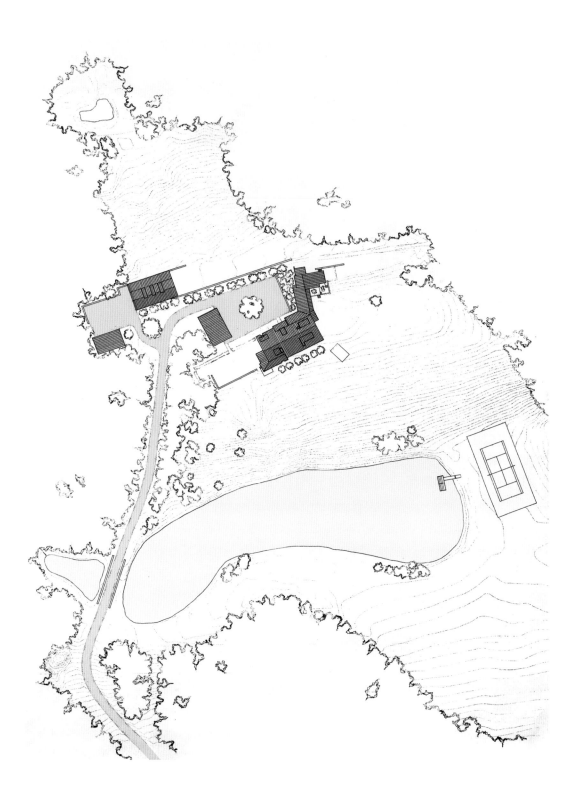

Site plan

Looking from breakfast terrace
toward tennis courts and lake

MOUNTAIN HOUSE   Covered dock with tennis courts   Stone and plank walk
                                               behind

View of house through landscape

39 <u>MOUNTAIN HOUSE</u>   North and east facades seen from
across lake

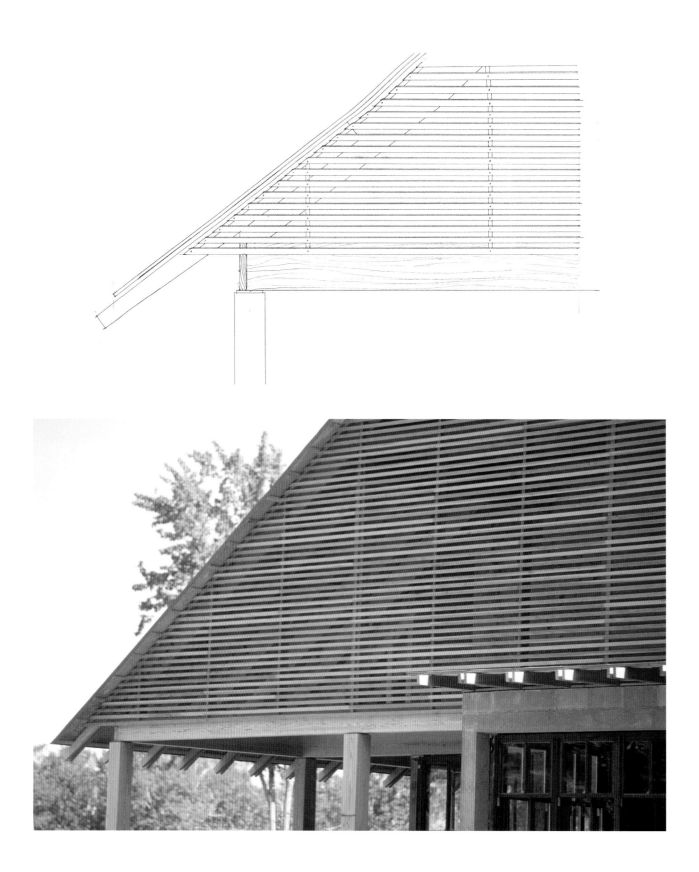

Slatted gable elevation detail

Slatted gable at dining room stone
porch

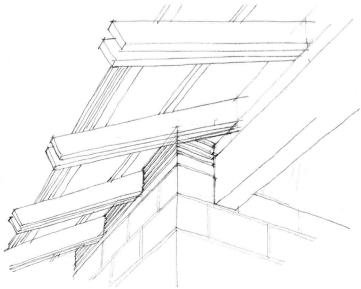

<u>MOUNTAIN HOUSE</u>   Eave detail   Eave detail

Stone porch adjacent to dining room

Glazed entry at dining room

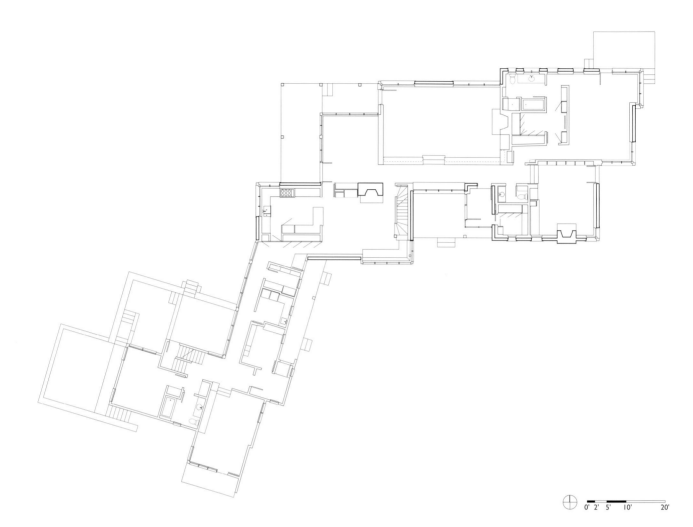

Upper corridor railing detail

View through living room to dining
room entry

Landscape view at stair hall

View looking north

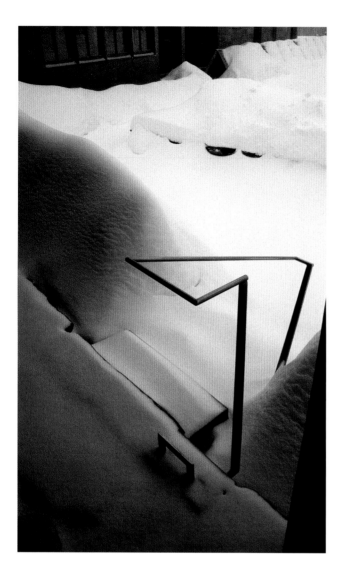

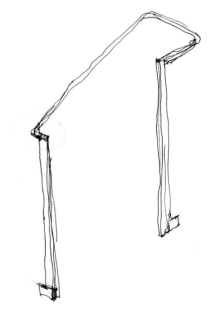

NEW YORK TOWNHOUSE

Having a strong appreciation for the Canadian Centre for Architecture, the clients commissioned this gut renovation in order to create a home with the appropriate atmosphere for their significant art collection.

The townhouse, originally built in 1918 and converted into an eight-unit apartment building in the 1940s, was returned to its original use as a single-family residence. While maintaining the clients' strong desire for privacy in their day-to-day lives and the ability to entertain in a relatively formal manner, the new house would also have to accommodate a significant art collection, providing museum quality environmental and lighting control.

Following the demolition of the 1940s apartment conversion, all that remained of the original townhouse was the limestone facade. This left the reconfiguration of space open to new organizing principles. The house is designed around two vertically stacked courts. The upper court, open to the sky, provides a secluded outdoor garden around which the family spaces are arranged. The lower interior court, sky-lit from the upper court, contains the main stair and is the focus of the entry, dining room, living room, and library. Asymmetrical in plan and split in section, this lower court offers diagonal views to the city and sky, bringing daylight into what is conventionally the darkest and most internalized portion of a New York City townhouse. A gentle atrium stair, with shallow rise to run ratio, allows easy ascent through the five main floors of the house.

The atrium stair is a complex piece of connective tissue that provides wide and narrow spaces, integrates wall art display and sculpture display with vertical and horizontal circulation, and deftly provides museum quality sound and air control. Treads span nearly the whole atrium at the bottom, then recede to a graceful band along the wall, opening the atrium to the light above. Choreography of the numerous elements was resolved by a simple and tireless commitment to drawing and redrawing, introducing incremental changes.

Front facade, oblique

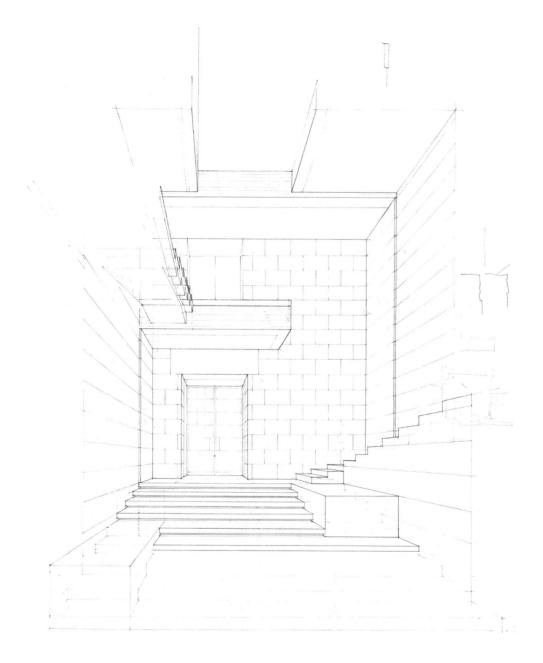

Atrium

Art display, atrium

Atrium, upper landing   Atrium stair detail   Atrium railing detail

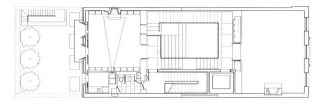

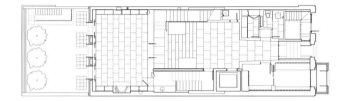

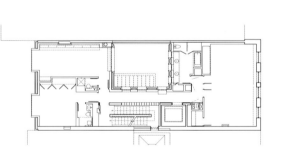

65 NEW YORK
    TOWNHOUSE

First floor plan   Third floor plan
Second floor plan   Fourth floor plan

Section, rendered study

Upper balcony, inner court

Library with hidden door to wet bar

Library

Existing facades, photo collage

73 <u>NEW YORK</u>
<u>TOWNHOUSE</u>

NEW YORK
TOWNHOUSE

Doorway from rear garden to
dining room

Bath sink detail

Casework and fireplace detail

ART STUDIO
AND RESIDENCE

Programmatically, the project was to design a two-bedroom house, three-car garage with attached guesthouse, and a painting studio for an artist, her husband, and their teenage daughter. However, first and foremost, the project was and is about an extraordinary landscape. Sited along a line of trees to the east, the house and studio sit on a high ridge, with spectacular twenty-mile views of rolling fields and mountains to the west and north, and shorter, but picturesque views into pasture to the south.

Approach to the site is via a long drive from the north. Well below the elevation of the house, this drive traverses a field, crosses a thick line of trees and ascends an adjacent meadow to the east. At the garage, one arrives in the first and more utilitarian, of two gravel courtyards. From here one begins to sense the vastness and power of the landscape beyond. Moving through the trees to the second courtyard, flanked by the house on the south and studio on the north, the project is revealed as a protagonist in the landscape—an activator of one of Connecticut's most majestic and panoramic vistas.

Operating in similar fashion to the second court, the buildings also frame and reveal the landscape in very particular and deliberate ways. An existing pair of stacked-stone walls define a fragment of an historic roadway, which formerly traversed the site. Taking this as a cue, two concrete frames were cast-in-place in parallel lines, creating the primary circulation spine for the main house. The house covers the frames as if they were its bones, but allows them to remain visible in fragments. Adjacent to the entry, a frame is reduced to knee height and continues from house into the landscape as a retaining wall. To move through the house, one either travels in parallel with, or crosses transversely through, the pair of concrete frames. When moving along the spine, telescopic long views are captured, emphasizing the landscape as a distant figure. Looking transversely, the concrete has an immediate presence, framing cross views of house and surroundings.

Materials are mostly concrete block, concrete, and cement board on the exterior of the buildings, and concrete, steel, and various woods (beech, mahogany, and fir) inside. As with the Mountain House (and in a more limited palate at Brookside Lower School at Cranbrook), the concrete block is made with a varied water mixture to provide individual blocks of varied tone. Used in careful juxtaposition to the silvered wood planks, cement board, and stone, a subtle palate is developed into which mahogany windows are set. The buildings are strong, tough, and deliberately restrained, a site-specific response always mindful and respectful of the powerful landscape.

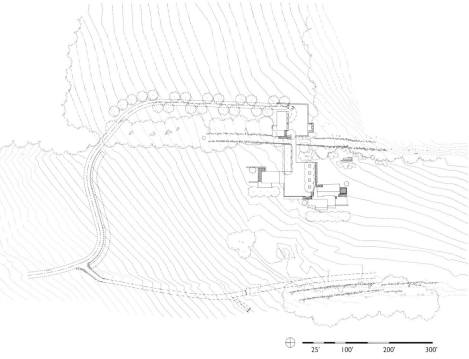

25'   100'   200'   300'

83   ART STUDIO
     AND RESIDENCE

South elevation   Site plan

Final approach, art studio on right,
main house left

Looking north toward art studio

Low
BRICK

0' 2' 5'   10'   20'

Schematic design site sketch   North elevation schematic design sketch

Concrete frame during construction   Concrete wall at entry with bar tie heads

Art studio

Concrete frame at main entry

Looking north from main entry

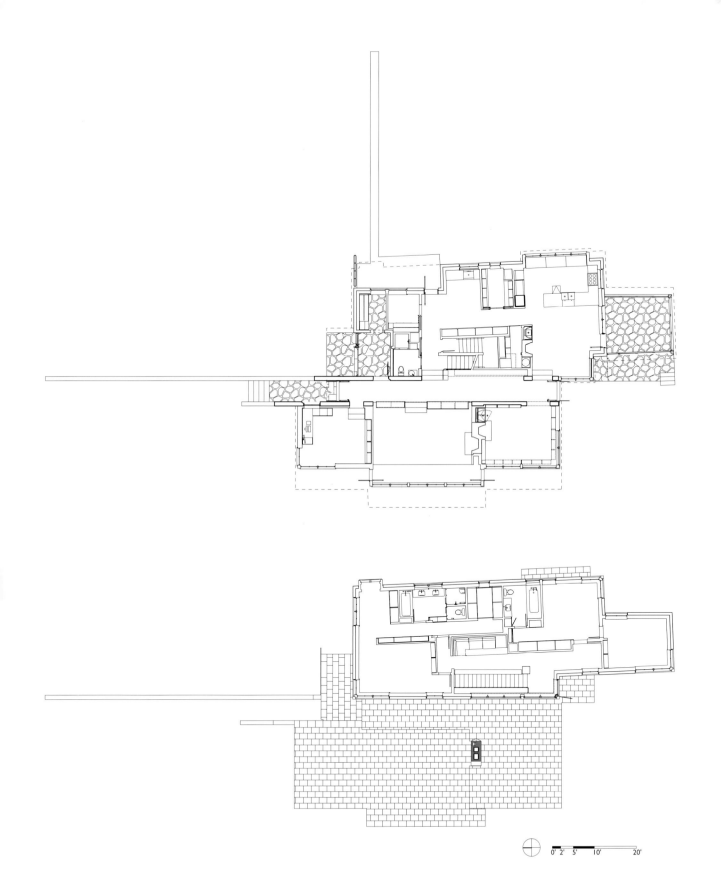

0' 2' 5' 10' 20'

**93 ART STUDIO
AND RESIDENCE**   Main floor plan study

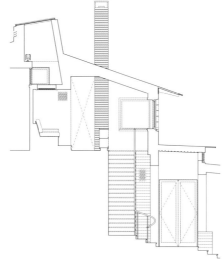

Main corridor, looking north   Stair and corridor section

ART STUDIO
AND RESIDENCE

Table with rice paper-laminated glass,
designed for house

View east from library, across main
corridor to kitchen

**97 ART STUDIO
AND RESIDENCE**

Looking north at library windows

VINEYARD RESIDENCE

The site is extraordinary—unlike any other on the island. The property is situated on a small peninsula, a bump on the coast, closer to the ocean than anyone will ever be able to build again. The views are breathtaking, over the ocean to the east, south, southwest, and over Stonewall Pond to the west. The southerly view is more than a mile of coastline—more than a mile of waves breaking against a magical, crescent-shaped shore of beaches and cliffs. The property has the front row seat to a million-acre ocean view.

Designed as a retreat for a New York art collector, the plan allows every room a view of the ocean. Windows facing the water are oversized, often going around corners to provide panoramic views of the coast. Every room has light and air from at least two, and often three sides. On bright days, the interior has balanced light and no glare, and even on the gloomiest days, lights will be rarely required anywhere in the interior. In the living room, dining room, kitchen, and study, large panels of glass slide open, eliminating all barriers to the sight, sound, and smell of the sea.

Cedar-planked walls are dimensioned to make space for cabinetry and the concealment of doors and sliding partitions. Interior doors swing into this space when open, becoming nearly invisible. Bedroom orientation provides complete visual privacy, so doors are rarely closed, and doorways remain open, cedar-planked passages. Entry and kitchen, and living room and office are separable by moving partitions, which slide or swing into wall spaces, concealing the partitions or cabinetry behind.

With a primary structure mostly of steel, the house is robust, constructed to weather well and be durable in the face of hurricanes and winter storms. At the same time, it is finely finished and detailed with both the exterior and interiors entirely of wood. Settled into its environment with a stubborn ruggedness, yet fully operable and made to engage the site by slipping out of the way, it is a carefully crafted piece of cabinetry, an instrument.

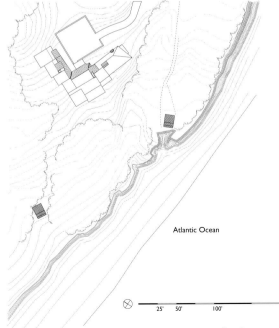

Atlantic Ocean

25' 50' 100' 200'

103 <u>VINEYARD RESIDENCE</u>   Dining room window with beach shack
beyond

Site plan

<u>VINEYARD RESIDENCE</u>   Southwest facade

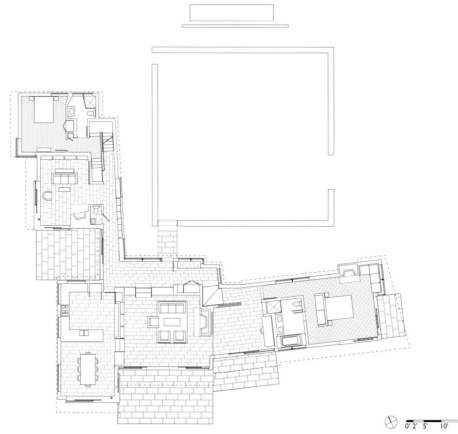

Northeast facade   Plan

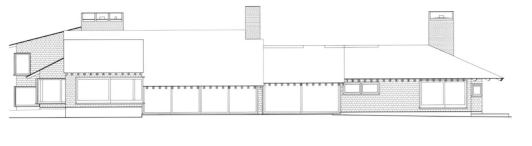

0' 2' 5'   10'   20'

0' 2' 5'   10'   20'

107 <u>VINEYARD RESIDENCE</u>   Southeast elevation   Entry section   Basswood site model detail

109 <u>VINEYARD RESIDENCE</u>   Operable vent windows at kitchen and
                                  dining room

<u>HOUSES</u> Operable corner windows
at library and bedroom above

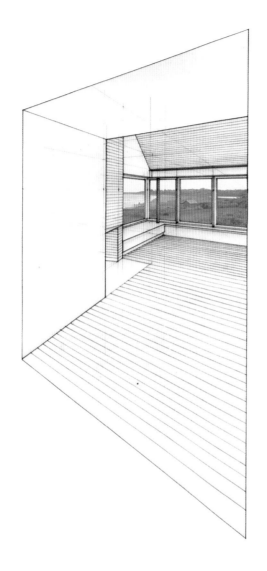

Perspective study, library   Perspective study, view from kitchen

Living room view   Study, beech casework

Living room vista through sliding
windows

Living room, entry, and study in background

Dining room view toward kitchen and
living room

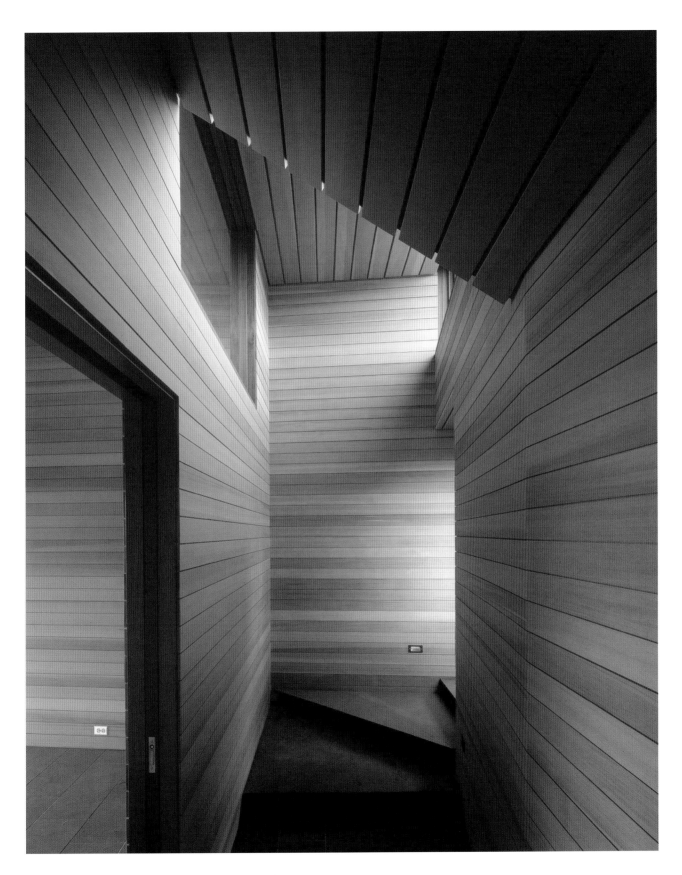

119 <u>VINEYARD RESIDENCE</u>   Planking at entry corridor

Planking at entry corridor

Bottom detail at corner of operable
window

123 <u>VINEYARD RESIDENCE</u>   Operable window at dining room

EAST HOUSE

Owners of a property adjacent to Vineyard Residence had to peek through windows before discovering a drawing scrap that revealed the architect's name, allowing them to schedule an interview, and ultimately initiate this project.

Nestled into the native shrubbery on the dynamic Martha's Vineyard coastline, East House's concrete facade welcomes the growth of local vines. Designed to meld into the vegetation and provide a robust face to New England's coastal weather, site-cast concrete is relieved with sustainably harvested Spanish cedar window frames. Without the sense of vernacular styling common to the previous houses, this project locates, across the landscape, a collection of concrete boxes whose orientation achieves both subtle and dramatic responses to the landscape.

During design, a commissioned study revealed a rate of coastal bluff erosion that made both client and architect extremely uncomfortable about the future of the residence. After much consideration, the solution was to cast the floors, formerly wood framed, in concrete, making each box a structural unit that could be individually lifted and moved to a location far from the bluff should erosion occur. The house is thus divided into concrete boxes, individually liftable with all interior finishes in place, and interstitial corridors, light wood framed zones that are easily removed and rebuilt in the event the building is moved.

Visitors arrive by a short drive through the oak, pine, and spruce forest, coming to park behind a concrete wall with a glimpse of the ocean beyond. A stair is tucked into the landscape near the wall (which is actually a side of the garage), and leads to a path through the trees.

Visible after a short walk, a concrete facade is parted by a glazed entry, and Douglas fir planking casts a warm interior glow in contrast to the concrete exterior. Constructed as six cast-in-place boxes with wooden liners, interior wall placement completes the figure begun by the exterior walls. Circulation travels along the interior figure of the boxes, through interstitial spaces both rough framed and finished in wood, and is choreographed to an ever more revealing experience of the site. Visitors are led south toward the library and living area, moderately close views of island shrubbery leading the way, while a tapering of the plan and a short stair in the opposite direction signal privacy and a bedroom wing to the north. Three gentle steps drop down a level, and the ceiling rises. Here tall sliding windows pull back completely within the concrete walls, removing from sight the linkage between boxes, and bringing a cross breeze through native spruces and pines. Continuing forward, glazing reveals a scattering of spruce and cedar trees with the ocean beyond.

Moving next into the living space, a daring cantilever spans the broad window opening, and an expanse of glass along five walls folds in and out between boxes to reveal a dramatic panorama of the sea. Operable windows pull back, and the gap amplifies the sound of the ocean, bringing it and sea breezes through the entire house. Geothermal wells use the earth's thermoconductivity to temper living spaces, vastly reducing the size and operating cost of HVAC equipment. With radiant heating, calibrated window openings, and the thermal mass of concrete, the house creates natural ventilation and buffers summer heat gain. Situated close into the greenery, it is nearly invisible from points further up the slope.

Site topography rendering

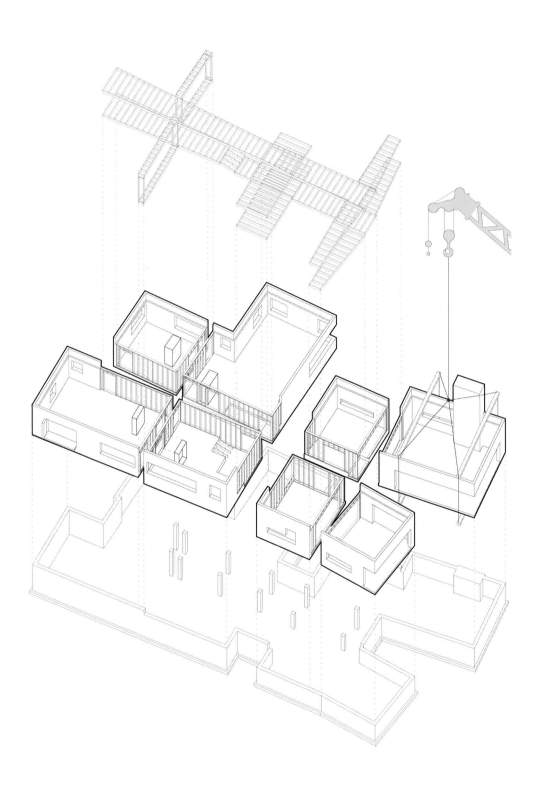

129 <u>EAST HOUSE</u>   Axonometric diagram showing discrete
and liftable concrete boxes.

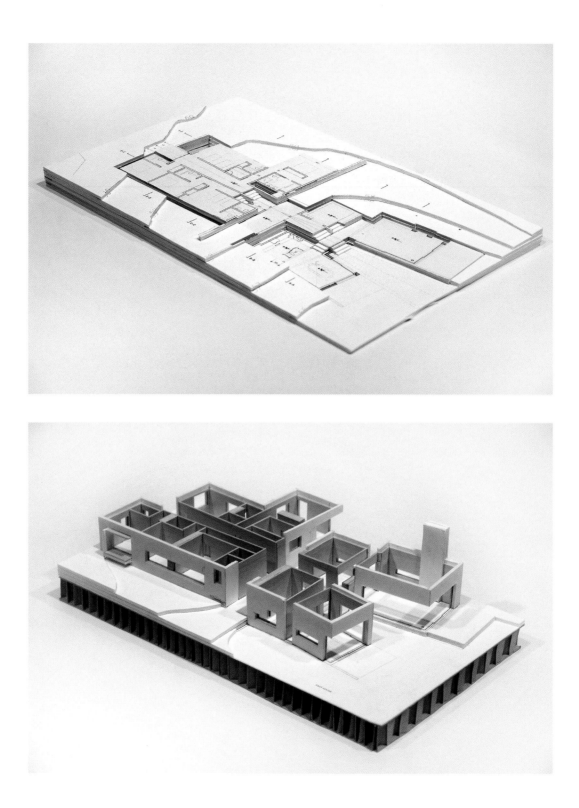

<u>HOUSES</u> Floor plan study model Concrete shell and wood liner study
model, roof removed

131 <u>EAST HOUSE</u>   Concrete shell and wood liner study
model, roof in place

133 <u>EAST HOUSE</u>

Exterior view of concrete shell and
planted roof, schematic study

<u>HOUSES</u> Spanish cedar window overlooking
main entry, construction photo

135 <u>EAST HOUSE</u>

Master bedroom with library in
background, construction photo

Master bedroom sliding glass door,
construction photo

137 <u>EAST HOUSE</u>

Kitchen and dining room facade showing interstitial sliding window between concrete boxes, construction photo

Oblique view across entry facade, construction photo

Main entry approach design study

EAST HOUSE   Main entry, design study

Entry corridor, design study

View from dining room toward living
area and landscape

View from living area toward dining
room, design study

View from dining room toward living
area and landscape

APPENDIX

KRIPALU HOUSING TOWER

Tucked into the trees of the Berkshire mountains, a range that links Art Studio and Residence and Mountain House to Rose's home mountains of Quebec, Kripalu Housing Tower is a conceptual link pointing from past work to the future of the architecture of Peter Rose. Essentially a big house, the eight-room residential dormitory at Kripalu Center for Yoga and Health creates for visitors and workshop attendees the same interrelationship between shelter and landscape that each of the houses explore, while serving its institutionally scaled program by the subtle integration of a series of domestically scaled spaces.

The design emerged in parallel to the development of East House, and the two projects share similarly sized plans, both organized along a tapering axis that both funnels breezes and captures landscape views. Each are integrated into the landscape with the simple and bold placement of concrete, wood, and glass, with each material designed to express its natural characteristics. Siting and plan decisions establish the buildings as places with deference to their contexts, and yet provide for visitors a vibrant and intimate connection to these natural surroundings in all seasons.

At Kripalu, concrete foundation and cores are expressed in juxtaposition to a slatted cypress-wood rain screen, which will weather to a natural gray, letting the lakeside building recede into the wooded context. A glazed passage with a planted roof and southern exposure provides a warm, bright connection for winter yogis moving between the Housing Tower and the existing retreat building during cold weather, yet the passage itself remains invisible from the garden just to the north. A slight bend in plan, which telegraphs from corridor wall to facade, directs guestroom views toward either the lake or the Berkshire hills, while editing adjacent buildings from view. As with the houses, no angle is accidental, and nearly every significant plan move can be traced to something in the site.

The building follows in the tradition of Cranbrook and the Milton Science project, reducing building design to a minimal practice that finds pleasure when using the properties of materials to respect and activate the valuable qualities of the context. As with East House, Kripalu Housing Tower does this with a straightforward palate, deftly integrated into the site. If East House is the Zen-like distillation of house to the point of invisibility, Kripalu paints this essence across eighty weekend monks' cells, making a second home for those on retreat, and reveals itself as a work with sensitivity to site, energy, and materials—pointing unequivocally to the future.

<u>HOUSES</u> East facade viewed through the land-
scape from main grounds approach

West elevation and main entrance in
afternoon sun

<u>HOUSES</u>   North stair tower and east facade with Berkshire hills in the distance   Close view of east facade and cypress slat corner detailing

North stair tower detail at west facing glazing

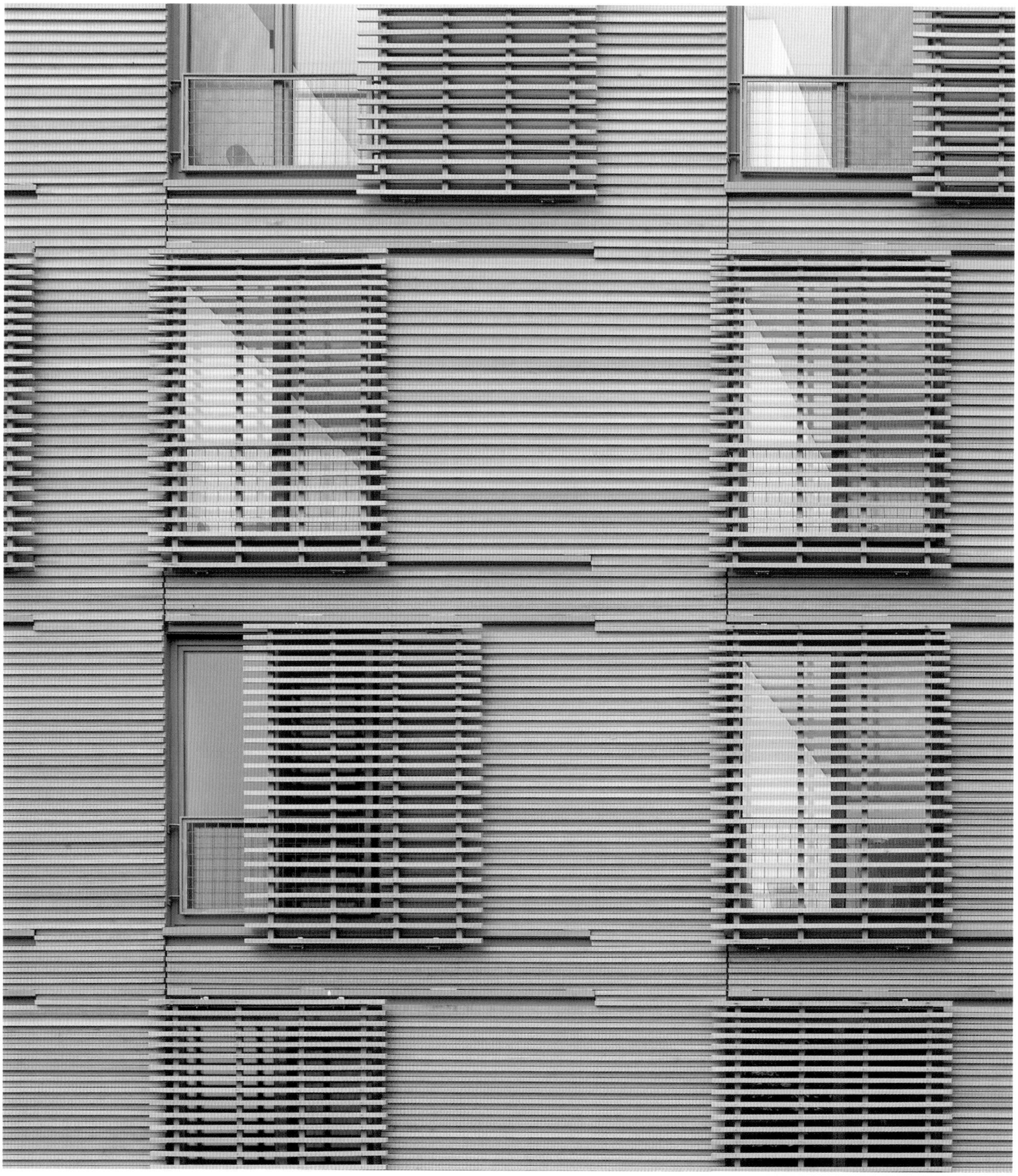

 West facade orthogonal detail

Cypress slats shedding rain drops,
southwest corner

Cypress slat detail, northeast corner

Dormitory with window view to Stockbridge Bowl

Dormitory view past sliding cypress screen to Stockbridge Bowl

153 APPENDIX KRIPALU HOUSING TOWER

1 View showing glazed partition and translucent curtain between sleeping room and shower

2 Locally fabricated, Peter Rose-designed hanger rack and wall hung bureau create a minimally appointed closet space while maximizing interior daylighting.

3 Glazed door and sidelight, glazed shower partition, and fully mirrored glass on the back wall allow light and exterior views from every angle in bathroom.

Views from stair tower landings are
always oriented to the landscape.

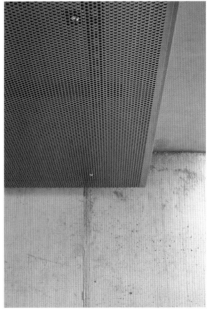

Main lobby, looking south from entry   Entry lobby ceiling services screen, detail

ACKNOWLEDGMENTS

The projects in this book were designed and constructed with the inspiration, help and collaboration of several people. I would like to thank the most important among them.

Two mentors have influenced me a great deal in executing this work. Rafael Moneo, who invited me to teach at the Graduate School of Design at Harvard in 1990, and is an architect and a human being I admire, like, and respect immensely. An intellectual as well as an artist, the energy, rigor, integrity, and dignity Rafael brings to everything he does, has been an inspiration. The wonderful Dan Kiley—with whom I had the privilege to collaborate for more than a decade before his death—opened my eyes to ways of looking at and thinking about buildings, sites, and landscapes. He was a delightful presence and influence in my working process.

In the office over the years, several key collaborators made it possible for the houses to be successfully developed, drawn, and built. James Dallmann and Jeff King were instrumental in the realization of the Vermont and Connecticut houses respectively. Tom Perkins, Jeremy Ficca, and Erkin Ozay played important roles on the first Martha's Vineyard house. Erkin Ozay and Matthew Snyder are in the process of bringing East House to completion. Paul Puciata deserves special mention for expertly and tirelessly running the extraordinarily complex Manhattan Townhouse project. I would like to express my specific gratitude to Matthew Snyder, who in addition to running projects over the last five years, has been an immense help to me and played a critical role in all aspects of the office, including the realization of this book.

Two brilliant collaborators outside the office deserve special thanks as well. My good friend Matthias Schuler, with whom I have worked on many projects over the last several years, has gradually helped me understand that making sustainable buildings is not only a moral responsibility, but that far better and interesting buildings are the result. Michael Van Valkenburgh—artist, thinker and worthy successor to the great Dan Kiley—has been exceptional to work with, particularly on East House, for which his insights have been exceptional.

It was William Morgan who suggested it was time to put these houses into a book, and his ability to provide a greater context to the work has been invaluable.

Lastly, I would like to thank Eve Blau, a wonderful architectural thinker, writer, and also my wife, who has helped me in incalculable ways.
—Peter Rose

OFFICE CREDITS

The coordination and follow through required to develop and represent these projects has rested, over the years, on the shoulders of an extremely capable office staff of architects and designers. Additionally, in this academic design environment, a cast of interns has been a constant source of talent and inspiration. Credit is due to the following architects, designers, and interns for their part in making possible the work shown here.

In chronological order
James Dallman, John McLaughlin, Paul Puciata, Jeff King, Martha Cassel, Kyle Larabee, Tom Perkins, Jennifer Minetree, Tamara Metz, William Bryant, Jay Valenta, Wendy Shlensky, Zeke Brown, Thomas Robinson, Beth Stadnicki, Wynne Mun, Lan Ying Ip, Michele Adrian, Yasmin Kuhn, Jeremy Ficca, Jane Ahn, Lola Sheppard, Adam Semel, Mark McGlothlin, Alastair Townsend, Mette Aamodt, David Choi, Ying Zhou, Karl Munkelwitz, Andrew Plumb, Abby Klima, Matthew Snyder, Elizabeth Richey, Duong Bui, Brian Baldor, Becky Hutchinson, Ramona Albert, Erkin Ozay, Jonathan Chace, Katherine Feather, Van Wilkes Fowlkes, Laura Crescimano, Louis Kraft, Shu Lai, and Grace Escano.

BIOGRAPHIES

PETER ROSE

Peter Rose is a recognized leader in the architectural design profession. Since beginning his practice in 1978, Rose has received numerous awards for residential, institutional, and urban design projects. His work ranges from large-scale urban design, such as the Old Port of Montreal Waterfront Master Plan, to smaller renovations and additions.

In 1989, after completing design and construction of the Canadian Centre for Architecture in Montreal, Rose was asked to teach at Harvard University's Graduate School of Design by then Architecture Department chair, José Rafael Moneo. He has since been Adjunct Professor of Architecture at the Graduate School of Design, and has also taught at Princeton University, McGill University, and at the University of Toronto.

He currently maintains an international practice in Cambridge, Massachussetts.

RAFAEL MONEO

Pritzker Prize recipient José Rafael Moneo is well known internationally for his distinguished career as architect and theoretician. Lecturing and publishing widely, as well as maintaining a broad and critically engaged architectural practice spanning over four decades, his work includes Kursaal Congress Centre in San Sebastian, Spain, and the Davis Museum and Cultural Center at Wellesley College in Massachusetts.

Formerly a fellow at the Spanish Academy in Rome, and the chairman of Harvard University's Graduate School of Design, Department of Architecture, from 1985 until 1990, he is currently the Josep Lluís Sert Professor of Architecture at the Harvard Graduate School of Design.

WILLIAM MORGAN

William Morgan is an architectural historian based in Providence, Rhode Island. He has taught at Princeton University, University of Louisville, and Brown University, and is the author of *Yankee Modern: The Houses of Estes/Twombly* and *The Cape Cod Cottage*.

PROFESSIONAL NOTES

SELECTED AWARDS

Small Firms Small Projects Design Awards, *Honor Award for Design Excellence*, Boston Society of Architects, 2007. Martha's Vineyard Residence

Small Firms Small Projects Design Awards, *Citation for Design*, Boston Society of Architects, 2007. Cloud Foundation Upgrade

New York Chapter Design Awards, American Institute of Architects, 2001. Manhattan Townhouse

New York Chapter Design Awards, American Institute of Architects, 2001. Mountain Residence

Award for Excellence, *Architectural Record* Record Houses, 1998. Mountain Residence

College of Fellows Medal, Royal Architectural Institute of Canada, 1994.

Medal of Excellence, Royal Architectural Institute of Canada, 1993. Canadian Centre for Architecture

Prix d'excellence, Urban Design, Ordre des Architectes du Québec, 1993. Le Vieux Port de Montréal Master Plan

National Honor Award, American Institute of Architects, 1992. Canadian Centre for Architecture

Progressive Architecture Urban Design Award, 1992. Le Vieux Port de Montréal Master Plan

Prix d'excellence, Ordre des Architectes du Québec, 1991. Le Centre Eaton

Prix d'excellence, Ordre des Architectes du Québec, 1989. Canadian Centre for Architecture

Award for Excellence, *Architectural Record* Record Houses, 1984. House on Lake Memphremagog

Architecture Quebec Design Award, 1982. Bradley House

Architecture Quebec Design Award, 1982. House on a Hill

Progressive Architecture Design Award, 1978. Pavillon Soixante-Dix

Design Award, Ordre des Architectes du Québec, 1978. Bradley House

SELECTED PUBLICATIONS

Moe, Kiel. *Thermally Active Systems in Architecture*. New York: Princeton Architectural Press, 2009.

Moe, Kiel. *Integrated Design in Contemporary Architecture*. New York: Princeton Architectural Press, 2008.

Meras, Phyllis. "Windows on Display." *Martha's Vineyard Magazine Home & Garden*, Fall 2007/Winter 2008.

Morgan, William. "Masterpiece Rooted in the Vineyard Landscape." *Providence Journal*, September 10, 2007.

Barbanel, Josh. "Moving In, Moving On." *The New York Times*, August 26, 2007.

Morgan, William. "Vineyard House Is Part of The Landscape." *Hartford Courant*, August 26, 2007.

Barbanel, Josh. "Big Deal: A Record FSBO?" *The New York Times*, July 15, 2007.

Faculty Project: Milton Science Building. *Harvard Design Magazine*, Fall 2006/Winter 2007.

Robertson, Robin. "The Vision Within Reach: A Milton Academy Distinguished for Creating Leaders in Science." *Milton Magazine*, Spring 2006.

Eck, Jeremiah. *The Face of Home: A New Way to Look at the Outside of Your House*. Newtown, CT: Taunton Press, 2006.

Kolleeny, Jane. "Art Studio and Residence." *Architectural Record*, January 2006.

Levinson, Nancy. "Stowe Away Home." *New England Home*, September–October 2005.

Paredes Benìtez, Cristina. *Luxury Houses: City*. New York: TeNeues Publishing Group, 2005.

Eck, Jeremiah. *The Distinctive Home: A Vision of Timeless Design*. Newtown, CT: Taunton Press, 2003.

Campbell, Robert. "Carpenter Center's Beautiful Intruder." *The Boston Globe*, August 25, 2002.